E. W. Syle

The Perpetuity of National Life

A Sermon, Delivered ... Dec. 7, 1865, in Christ Church, Pelham, N.Y

E. W. Syle

The Perpetuity of National Life
A Sermon, Delivered ... Dec. 7, 1865, in Christ Church, Pelham, N.Y

ISBN/EAN: 9783337116217

Printed in Europe, USA, Canada, Australia, Japan

Cover: Foto ©Lupo / pixelio.de

More available books at **www.hansebooks.com**

The Perpetuity of National Life.

A

SERMON,

DELIVERED ON THANKSGIVING DAY,

THURSDAY, DEC. 7, 1865,

IN CHRIST CHURCH, PELHAM, N. Y.,

BY THE

REV. E. W. SYLE, A. M., RECTOR.

PRINTED BY REQUEST.

New York:

JAS. W. TRUBSHAW, BOOK & JOB PRINTER,
58 FULTON STREET.

1865.

PELHAM, WESTCHESTER Co.. Dec. 15th, 1865.

REV. E. W. SYLE.

Rev. and Dear Sir:—Several of your parishioners, to whom the Sermon preached by you on last Thanksgiving Day (and repeated by request on the following Sabbath) was most acceptable, as being eminently appropriate to the occasion, and to the present condition of our country, have expressed a desire that the Christian and patriotic sentiments inculcated in it should be more widely disseminated, by its publication in pamphlet form. We would therefore request (if entirely agreeable to yourself) that you will enable us to gratify this wish, by furnishing us with the manuscript of your Sermon, for that purpose.

We are, Rev. and Dear Sir,

Respectfully, your sincere friends,

R. EMMET,
WM. HENRY LEROY,
JOHN FOWLER, Jr.,
D. CHERBULIEZ,
ROBT. W. EDGAR.

PELHAM PRIORY, 20th Dec., 1865.

MESSRS. R. EMMET, WM. H. LEROY,
and others.

My Dear Friends and Parishioners:—Your gratifying request can hardly receive any other reply than a ready assent. And yet the difference between the impression made by a Discourse delivered to an attached congregation, and that of the same words when merely read by others, is great enough to make one pause before *printing* what he is quite ready to *preach*. At the same time, I do not hesitate to avow that I regard the views and principles of my Sermon as important; and if you judge them adapted to be useful in pamphlet form, the manuscript is at your service for the purpose of publication.

Believe me to be,

With sincere regard, your Friend and Pastor,

E. W. SYLE.

SERMON.

"Only take heed to thyself, and keep thy soul diligently, lest thou forget the things which thine eyes have seen: and lest they depart from thy heart all the days of thy life; but teach them thy sons, and thy sons' sons."—DEUT. 4:9.

THERE are times when events speak for themselves: and there are states of feeling which are spontaneous—requiring no arguments to produce them, but almost resenting any attempt to heighten their intensity by mere use of words.

What captive, just set free, would care to hear a dissertation on the blessings of liberty, or the duty of feeling happy? What convalescent needs to have the advantages of health demonstrated to his understanding, or the joyous feeling of returning strength urged upon him as a matter of duty? What mariner who finds refuge in a safe harbor, after a perilous storm, wants to be told that it is a good thing to be preserved from shipwreck, or that it is proper for him to experience a feeling of relief?

It would be counted an impertinence to obtrude such counsels at such times; and the effect of attempting it would be to cause a revulsion of thought

and feeling quite contrary to what may have been de-
signed and desired. Not less incongruous, dear Christian friends, would it be, on such an occasion as this,
to present an array of facts bearing on the reasons
that exist for national thankfulness, or to demonstrate
that the feeling of gratitude to the King of Kings
ought to fill the heart of every worshipper in this
house to-day.

We *are* thankful: it is a matter of the simplest
consciousness with us; needing no demonstration and
admitting of no argument. We *know* we have reason
to feel this gratitude; so that we want no one to tell
us what we all so instinctively understand and ap-
preciate.

What then shall be the subject of our remarks on
this auspicious day? Shall we have nothing to say,
one to another, concerning the perils of the past, and
the blessings of the present hour? Shall we content
ourselves with the simple enjoyment of our delive-
rances and exemptions; and take no thought for the
coming years; but trust that the powerful hand which
has so signally sustained and guided thus far, will
still sustain and guide in all future emergencies?

Such trust we well may cherish; and in proportion
as it is a simple and well-placed confidence in the God
and Father of us all, and is not a mere blind, unrea-
soning hopefulness, we shall be ready to give heed to
what God himself has spoken to a people who had
just been brought through great troubles, and had
experienced a wonderful deliverance.

Just eighty years before, the same Moses, through
whom these words were addressed to the Jewish nation, had made his first essay for their deliverance—

thinking they would understand his purpose and welcome him as their prince and champion; but their minds were not prepared; they were comparatively content with their condition; they preferred the flesh-pots of Egypt to the prospect of emancipation; and Moses fled away from them and from Pharaoh, finding in Midian a refuge and a home; so that for forty long years he sojourned there, keeping the flock of Jethro, his father-in-law, and (as we suppose) composing the most ancient work extant, and one of the most sublime of all poems—the book of Job: a production worthy of a scholar, a hero, a genius, and a legislator! and Moses was all these.

After the forty years thus well spent, after that maturity of mind had been developed which constituted the providential preparation for his future work, then came the alarming summons to undertake the leadership of that down-trodden people who had previously refused his aid, and whose condition had become ten-fold worse than before—with this exception, that, whereas formerly they had not been ready to accept deliverance, now they sighed by reason of their bondage, and their cry came up unto God by reason of their bondage, for it was very sore.

We will not trace out the steps of their exodus from Egypt, nor dwell upon their faithless and faint-hearted shrinking from the Divine directions given to them, nor will we delineate the provocations which marked their weary wandering in the wilderness for another forty long years. Enough, that during all this time, Moses was their leader, and that he brought them once again to the very borders of the promised land, and gave to the new generation that had sprung up a new and fuller declaration of the laws of God—adding his own earnest exhortations and solemn warnings.

How far his prophetic eye penetrated the obscurity of the remote future, or how far it was mere human sagacity which prompted his forebodings, it is plain that he anticipated for the people of his care anything but an untroubled career. The great alternatives of obedience with prosperity on the one hand, and of disobedience with destruction on the other, were so plainly, so strongly, so repeatedly put before them, that we, who read these things in the light of the subsequent sorrows which mark the Jewish history, wonder at the little heed they gave to the counsels—so profoundly wise, as well as so tenderly affectionate—of the venerable chief to whom they owed so much. But—alas for them, and for the world!—those words of wisdom were disregarded; and the nation that had been so miraculously delivered and so marvellously preserved; so carefully instructed and so signally blessed; at last brought ruin upon themselves by neglecting that which, had they observed, the glory of God's chosen people, instead of their shame, would have been recorded on the page of history; they would have been recognized universally as chief among the nations, and their capital as the joy of the whole earth !

They had been, at the period when our text was spoken, brought through all their difficulties; their experiences had been varied and animating; under almost every form of trial they had been sustained; but there remained for them much yet to accomplish—even the entire subjugation of the iniquitous Canáanites; and the more difficult task of resisting the idolatrous allurements which would beset them when they should be fully established in the promised land. It was in view of these things that Moses exhorted them in the words of our Text—"only *take heed*," said he. "Be not careless and confident concerning thyself, as though it were guaranteed that thou shouldest never err. Keep thy soul diligently: let not other things interfere with chief attention to those things which thine eyes have seen. Nay: let these be *life-long* subjects of meditation; and, moreover, teach them to thy children, and to *their* children also; lest they, being ignorant, uninstructed, uninformed, fall into great troubles, and experience afresh those miseries of the past from which thou hast been thyself delivered: let them be spared this renewal of your sorrows."

This last consideration is that on which we would particularly dwell—the duty of instructing the young in the lessons of the past; of instilling into their minds true principles on *all* subjects, not counting it a matter of indifference "what the children think," but realizing and remembering that the seeds of thought sown in the minds of our children (yes, and of our little grandchildren), are *sure* to germinate there, and to bear fruit in due season—perhaps long after we ourselves have passed away; but *perhaps, on the other hand, much sooner than any of us would anticipate!*

The life-time of one generation is long enough to develop a harvest of mischief which a whole nation may reap to their sorrow. Thirty or forty years ago, and the greater part of those who have striven and suffered in the great national struggle were mere children—and not a small proportion of them little babes in their mothers' arms ; nay, half that number of years has sufficed to determine the character and form the opinions of perhaps the most efficient elements of those armies which have engaged in mortal strife—some surviving ; but many, oh, how many ! going down to premature and bloody graves.

And how were these taught ? Where did they imbibe the principles which led to these results ? What was the nature of the education which prepared them for the emergency that called for action ? It was not the stately teachings of the college professor —though these had their proportionate effect ; it was not the careful instructions of the regular school, though these also exercised a large influence in their way ; it was not even the more authoritative declarations of the pulpit, though these gave their sanction to the broad general principles which embrace all moral questions. *More* than all these—more in number, and greater in influence—were the unobserved, informal, unconscious teachings and learnings that went on by the fireside and at the dinner-table, in the nursery and on the play-ground, over the daily newspaper and the published census, at the political meeting and at the flag-raising ; by the anniversary oration and by the pungent pamphlet ; on the steamboat and rail-car, in the village lyceum and at the corners of the streets—on these, and many other like occasions, were the opinions formed and the courses of action resolved upon, which culmina- .

ted in that stupendous outburst of war, for the cessation of which we are this day assembled to return thanks to Him who is at once the God of battles and the Prince of Peace. It was by means of that unceasing indoctrination which always goes on when men are in earnest on any subject, that those great results have been reached, the magnitude and importance of which have fixed the gaze of the astonished world. It was not the phrenzy of a moment, but the determination of those who had been prepared for the part they sustained by life-long teachings and innumerable influences; it was by that process which Moses both describes and enjoins when he says—"Thou shalt teach them diligently unto thy children, and shalt talk of them when thou sittest in thine house, and when thou walkest by the way, and when thou liest down, and when thou risest up." (Deut. vi. 7.)

Had such diligence and earnestness been exhibited in the inculcation of right principles of national duty and national morality, throughout the whole nation during the past thirty years, what might not have been spared to this generation! And if the *next* generation is to be spared the like sufferings, it must be by more diligence and less indifference on the part of those who now see and feel how great a price has been paid for the perpetuation of those national blessings that have been imperilled. Foolish notions must not be allowed to pass unchallenged and uncontradicted, for they will increase unto more unreasonableness; and there is nothing too foolish for men to take up with, who are determined to carry their point at all hazards. False philosophizings must be exposed, and not treated as mere whims of no practical bearing : the effect of philosophically *regarding* a given race of men as *essentially* inferior is practically to *treat* them as essentially inferior. Fallacious theories must not be laughed at as simply amusing : but must be exploded as dangerous and destructive. Unwarranted assumptions must not be put up with as harmless peculiarities ; but resisted as threatening the liberties of those committed to our charge. For we are indeed the Trustees of coming generations ; and it becomes us to guard, with a holy jealousy, against the insidious approaches of mischief; and to count nothing harmless which carries with it the seeds of error.

All this involves trouble, and pains-taking, and self-denial ; according to that true saying, " Unceasing vigilance is the price of liberty ;" and in a country like this, where the ultimate decision of all questions rests on the will of the people, the exercise of this attribute of sovereignty implies a weighty responsibility, and demands an amount of thought and effort commensurate with the greatness of the trust so exercised.

It is not permitted for the people of a republican government to be inert or unconcerned about the principles and practices which prevail around them. In other lands, where privileged ranks and ruling classes are recognized, there may be some consistency in allowing those to whom the task of ruling is a sort of inheritance, to take charge—as it were—of the common weal ; and the masses of the people may content themselves with simply giving their vote, if they have one, or only praying for their rulers, if they have not—trusting to the good providence of God, that He will promote to posts of influence men who will "execute justice and maintain truth;" at the same time looking, so far as human considerations come in, to the mutual watchfulness of parties, and to the effect of counter-balancing interests, for the prevention of any extreme deviation from the principles of good government.

But in a Republic the case is otherwise. The responsibilities of the position occupied by every voter cannot be devolved: they must be met and fulfilled; faithfully, industriously, and fearlessly; or else that power, which is always creeping from the many to the few, will be exercised by those who—for whatever reason—are found willing to give their time and attention to this especial work; and *they* will direct the energies, and *they* will apply the resources, of the people in accordance with their own ideas, or their calculations of present interest.

In this way many years of prosperity may pass, and the affairs of a nation may seem to go on sufficiently well, especially if there be large material resources at command, and population does not tread on the heels of production; but if a crisis arises; if selfishness, or self-will gain the ascendancy, and the influential actors of the day be willing to "give to party what was meant for man;" if "a factious band agree—to call it freedom when themselves are free;" if passion takes the place of principle, and contrivance of conscience, then the consequences are felt of having the

places of authority and influence occupied by men
who misrepresent the mind of the people; then the
nation is thrown into a convulsion, and it is only
after an agonizing struggle that the ultimate authority regains that practical control of affairs with
which it ought never to have parted.

What remains to be done thenceforward is to
guard against the recurrence of such a catastrophe,
though the right may have triumphed, and the vic-
tory be complete and glorious.

Would not the mariner, saved from shipwreck, na-
turally warn those who follow him against the errors
in navigation which jeopardized his vessel ? Would
he not also point out those excellent qualities of the
staunch ship which enabled it to outlive the storm ?
And if he desired to " point a moral or adorn a tale;"
would he not show his children how that noble struc-
ture was the result of thought, and skill, and patient
workmanship continued through months, it may be
years, of toil, and time, and perseverance ?

Yes : the exigencies of the moment bring into play
the energies and the accumulations of many generations ; and it depends upon the fidelity and industry
with which the work of our quiet years has been per-
formed, what shall be the issue of that strife—
whether it be of the elements or of the human pas-
sions—which may itself be a turning-point in the
history of a ship's crew, or of a nation's welfare, or
of the human race itself.

Such a contest has just now terminated. The ac-
cumulated teachings and workings of some fifty years
have been gradually increasing in strength and inten-

sity, and at last concentrated their force, on the one side and on the other, until not only did the heavens gather blackness, and the atmosphere become surcharged with the flashing fluid that destroys, and yet purifies; but the very earth beneath our feet trembled, and many of the old foundations were shaken down during the continuance of this unprecedented storm. But now that the fury of the tempest has spent itself, and the skies begin to look clear again, and the air is fresh and invigorating, and the earth feels firm once more, and we look abroad again— what do we behold? We see that the *area of human freedom has been marvellously enlarged*, and that the Great Republic of the West has, in its onward march kept step with the great northern monarchy, so that *Serf* and *Slave* are words of the past, and *Peasant* and *Freedman* take their place.

Well does the President indicate this as among the chief subjects for our thanksgiving! Its influence upon the great question of human enfranchisement from every form of bondage who can describe, or even conjecture! Compared with this, even those other blessings enumerated in the Proclamation—relief from the scourge of civil war; the securing of peace, unity and harmony; exemption from the calamities of foreign war, pestilence and famine; and the bestowment of the fruits of an abundant harvest —even these, great as they are, and deeply grateful as we should be for their enjoyment, hardly equal, in the comparison, that which is at once an enfranchisement both to master and to servant, and also a deliverance from evils the effects of which increased with each succeeding generation.

One other feature in the Thanksgiving Proclamation attracts our attention; and that is the prominent
recognition of the Divine dogma concerning government: " Righteousness exalteth a nation; but Sin is
a reproach to any people."

Oh, that this were not only recognized, but remembered—so remembered as to be steadily acted upon!
Not the number, in millions, of square miles; not the
hundreds of thousands of population; not the min-
eral wealth, unexhausted and even unexplored; not
the abundant productions of the earth, nor the
varied results of mechanic skill; not the prodigious
tonnage of shipping, nor the force of batteries, nor
the size of armies; not even the general intelligence
and intellectual culture of the people—none of these
constitute, though they all enhance, the exaltation of
a people: *that* is the office of righteousness alone—
of truth, and justice, of equal law, and of national
honor in its truest and noblest sense.

And these are the principles and sentiments we
are called upon to teach our children, and our children's children—acknowledging, as truth may require,
the national sins, in respect to these things, against
God's infinite goodness; acknowledging also that it is
not in man that walketh to direct his steps; and,
therefore, "imploring the divine guidance in the
ways of national virtue and holiness."

These are weighty words, coming as they do, from
the Chief Magistrate of the nation at such a time as
this. We trust, that, in proportion to the greater
reality and earnestness which characterize these days
as compared with the times preceding, will be the

sincerity of that regard which men will pay to this
immutable law of the Divine Government. "Righteousness exalteth a nation, but sin is a reproach to
any people."

Then the National Banner of these United States
will be recognized, the world over, as the Symbol of
Liberty conjoined with Law, of Progress guided by
Discretion, and of Intelligence ennobled by Religion.
It will be in the van-guard of a Christian civilization
which will carry the results of modern science to the
far-off nations whose advancement is checked by abso-
lutism in government, restriction in commerce, and
corruption in social life. It will be a token of encouragement to nations still struggling for the possession and enjoyment of free institutions; while it
will be a warning to all rulers who care more for the
pre-eminence of the few, than for the welfare of the
many. As it floats over scores of Consulates in foreign lands, it will be the symbol of good neighbor-
ship among nations, and at the same time a reminder
of the mischief of intermeddling with the interests
of others. As it flies from the mast-heads of hundreds of ships—both of war and commerce—whose
keels plough every sea, it will be an "ensign to the
nations from far," the meaning of which will be
"fair treaties and free commerce among all countries."
And now that in a sense which never before was
fully realized; now that, in truth, that flag does—
" Wave o'er the land of the *free*, and the home of the
brave," now let every heart resolve to support and sustain, defend and promulgate all those high principles
of which it is the beautiful and significant symbol;

making it the standard of a true crusade against
everything mean and ignoble, selfish and tyrannous;
until righteousness shall be established in the earth,
even until God shall "shake all nations, and the desire of all nations shall come."

It is a favorite device with some writers on government to trace an analogy between the life of a nation
and that of an individual; and to insist that as there
is in the one case youth and manhood, decadence
and death, so there must needs be in the other a rise
and progress, a decline and fall.

The idea is poetical, and does not lack some sem-
blance of confirmation from the history of the past
—Assyria, Babylon, Persia, Egypt, Greece, Rome,
Venetia—all have gone through this process, as
some would think completely; yet when we look
more closely, it is only the two first—Assyria and
Babylon—that have indeed become nationally extinct.
Persia is yet a nation; Egypt still gives signs of life:
and though the poet sang:

" 'Tis Greece
" But living Greece no more,"

that home of liberty and literature has still a flame
burning on its national altar. May it never be ex-
tinguished! Even Rome—old, glorious Rome—sur-
vives; and were it once delivered from sacerdotal
usurpation, who doubts but that she would yet lift
her head as the natural and rightful mistress of all
Italy?—a *nation* still, though not a popedom! And
beautiful Venetia is not dead; rather, as another
captive Briseis, the Austrian Agamemnon and the

Italian Achilles are contending for her possession. Nay; we might even reconsider our first concession, and say that if Bagdad be considered as supplementing Babylon, then the Caliph Omar revived the realm of Queen Semiramis, and we have yet a living representative among the nations, of the empire which Nimrod founded, and the city which Asshur went forth to build.

So fanciful and unfounded is that supposed analogy on which is based the expectation that nations must need decay and die.

Rather let the progress of a nation—and of *this* nation in particular—be compared to "the path of the just, which shineth more and more unto the perfect day." *Why not*—when it is possessed of that knowledge of sacred truth and saving righteousness which are the very salt of preservation, effectually counteracting the tendencies to corruption which, if unchecked, might end in extinction? Well may we look for this perpetuity, as a result of knowing and obeying all the Divine Law, when we see that the unremitting obedience to only *one* of the Ten Commandments—"Honor thy father and thy mother"— has brought down the promised blessing, and caused the people of the far-off land of Sinim to "dwell long in the land" which the Lord God in his providence gave them; so that they are now, not only the most *ancient* nation on the face of the earth, dating back consecutively to the times just subsequent to the flood, but are also the most *numerous* of all people; reckoning their four hundred millions of living souls!

Let this one example incite emulation, as well as

afford encouragement. Let *this* nation also become eminent for the degree in which father and mother are honored, let the whole code of righteousness be observed which truly exalteth a nation, and there will be no decay, no leading into captivity, no wasting and destruction in our fields; no complaining in our streets; but in place thereof joy and gladness, prosperity and perpetuity.

On the contrary: if the admonition of God's prophet and lawgiver be disregarded—if we take not heed to ourselves, and keep not our soul diligently; but forget the things which our eyes have seen, so that they depart from our hearts; if we teach them not to our children and our children's children—then there may come upon us—no; it will not be on *us*, but upon *them*—on the children of whose happiness we are the Guardians, and on the generations yet unborn for whose welfare we are the Trustees—on *them* will come the miseries which our fidelity might have averted.

The solemnity of so weighty a charge may well temper the joyousness of this happy day; though it ought not to overcloud the brightness of our rejoicing. It is hard to draw comparisons between this, and those former occasions in the nation's history, when peace and good-will have been restored after warfare and animosity; but the proportions of this latest strife, the aggravated nature of the contest, the unnaturalness of the circumstances, the obstinacy of the resistance, and the completeness of the defeat, all mark this as the most signal of all victories ever granted to this people. And, whereas, in other conflicts, especially in ancient times, the greatness of the triumph was enhanced by the numbers who had lost their freedom and passed into captivity; this—altogether on the contrary—is signalized by the unprecedented numbers who are *delivered* from the yoke of bondage and made free, so that they can call their bodies as well as their souls *their own.*

Now could that bell which hangs over Independence Hall, in Philadelphia, be rung so that its tones would be heard over the whole country, it might perform what is directed by the legend cast into its very substance; that almost prophetic passage from the book of Leviticus: "Proclaim Liberty throughout *all* the land, unto *all* the inhabitants thereof." Oh, that it might be to every one individually, that liberty wherewith Christ maketh free all that come unto the Father through him!

NOTE.

A portion of the last paragraph of Daniel Webster's letter, written in 1850, to certain citizens of Staunton, Virginia, is too illustrative not to be here added.

"Let me ask you to teach your young men, into whose hands the power of the country must soon fall, to go back to the close of the Revolutionary war; to contemplate the feebleness and incompetency of the confederation of States then existing; and to trace the steps by which the intelligence and patriotism of the great men of that day led the country to the adoption of the existing Constitution. Teach them to study the proceedings, votes and reports of committees in the old Congress. Especially draw their attention to the leading part taken by the Assembly of Virginia from 1783 onward. Direct their minds to the Convention at Annapolis in 1786; and by the contemplation and study of these events and these efforts, let them see what a mighty thing it was to establish the government under which we have now lived so prosperously and so gloriously for sixty years."

Works of Daniel Webster, Vol. VI, p. 581.

www.ingramcontent.com/pod-product-compliance
Lightning Source LLC
Chambersburg PA
CBHW031157090426
42738CB00008B/1378